UNDERSTANDING MYTHS

EGYPTIAN MYTHS

SHERI DOYLE

Crabtree Publishing Company

www.crabtreebooks.com

Author: Sheri Doyle

Publishing plan research and development:
Sean Charlebois, Reagan Miller
Crabtree Publishing Company

Editor-in-chief: Lionel Bender

Editors: Simon Adams, Lynn Peppas

Proofreaders: Laura Booth, Wendy Scavuzzo

Project coordinator: Kathy Middleton

Photo research: Kim Richardson

Designer: Ben White

Cover design: Margaret Amy Salter

Production coordinator and Prepress technician:
Margaret Amy Salter

Production: Kim Richardson

Print coordinator: Katherine Berti

Consultants: Noreen Doyle, M.A. Egyptology, M.A. Nautical Archaeology, B.A. Anthropology, Art, and Classical Civilizations: Author and consultant, Maine; and Amy Leggett-Caldera, M.Ed., Elementary and Middle School Education Consultant, Mississippi State University.

Cover: Sphinx and the Great Pyramid in the Egypt (top); statue of Egyptian feline goddess "Bastet" (bottom left and right); The Weighing of the Heart from the Book of the Dead of Ani (bottom center)

Title page: A colored stone relief on display at Deir el-Bahri, Egypt

Photographs and reproductions:

Maps: Stefan Chabluk

Front cover: Eternal Egypt: Masterworks of Ancient Art from the British Museum by Edna R. Russmann/ Wikimedia Commons: bottom center; Shutterstock: top and bottom left and right

The Art Archive: 18b (Bibliothèque Musée du Louvre/Gianni Dagli Orti), 21 (Musée du Louvre Paris/Gianni Dagli Orti), 22b (Gianni Dagli Orti), 24 (Egyptian Museum Cairo/Gianni Dagli Orti), 26b (Egyptian Museum Cairo/Gianni Dagli Orti), 31 (Musée du Louvre Paris/Gianni Dagli Orti), 34b (Egyptian Museum Cairo/Gianni Dagli Orti), 38 (Egyptian Museum Cairo/Gianni Dagli Orti). • Getty Images: 16 (Dorling Kindersley), 40. • The Kobal Collection: 44t (Alphaville/ Imhotep Prod). • shutterstock.com: 1 (PRILL Mediendesign und Fotografie), 4 (Sadequl Hussain), 4–5 (Vladimir Korostyshevskiy), 5 (Skripko Ievgen), 6 (Maugli), 6–7 (Kokhanchikov), 10t (Paul Vinten), 10b (King Tut), 10m (diez artwork), 13b (Steve Heap), 13m (Boris15), 14–15 (Dudarev Mikhail), 15b (Pius Lee), 18t (Sethislav), 19 (Doctor Jools), 20 (Netfalls), 22m (Doctor Jools), 24t (RBGrover), 40t (Vladimir Wrangel), 41l (S.Borisov), 41r (Elena Ray), 43t (Loskutnikov), 43m (Nikolai Tsvetkov), 43b, 44b (airphoto.gr). • Topfoto (The Granger Collection): 8–9, 17, 28, 33, 37; (topfoto.co.uk): 9 (ullsteinbild), 11 (ullsteinbild), 12, 13br (World History Archive), 27 (World History Archive), 30, 34t, 42. • Werner Forman Archive: 29 (Egyptian Museum, Cairo), 32t (Egyptian Museum, Cairo(, 32b (E. Strouhal).

This book was produced for Crabtree Publishing Company by Bender Richardson White

---

Library and Archives Canada Cataloguing in Publication

Doyle, Sheri
    Understanding Egyptian myths / Sheri Doyle.

(Myths understood)
Includes index.
Issued also in electronic formats.
ISBN 978-0-7787-4508-2 (bound).--ISBN 978-0-7787-4513-6 (pbk.)

    1. Mythology, Egyptian--Juvenile literature. 2. Egypt--Religion-Juvenile literature. I. Title. II. Series: Myths understood

BL2441.3.D69 2012   j299'.3113   C2011-908367-1

Library of Congress Cataloging-in-Publication Data

Doyle, Sheri.
    Understanding Egyptian myths / Sheri Doyle.
        p. cm. -- (Myths understood)
    Includes index.
    ISBN 978-0-7787-4508-2 (reinforced library binding : alk. paper) -- ISBN 978-0-7787-4513-6 (pbk. : alk. paper) -- ISBN 978-1-4271-7901-2 (electronic pdf) -- ISBN 978-1-4271-8016-2 (electronic html)
    1. Mythology, Egyptian--Juveline literature. 2. Egypt--Religion--Juvenile literature. I. Title.

BL2441.3.D695 2012
299'.3113--dc23
                                        2011050090

Crabtree Publishing Company

Printed in Canada/012012/MA20111130

www.crabtreebooks.com   1-800-387-7650

Published in Canada
Crabtree Publishing
616 Welland Ave.
St. Catharines, Ontario
L2M 5V6

Published in the United States
Crabtree Publishing
PMB 59051
350 Fifth Avenue, 59th Floor
New York, New York 10118

Published in the United Kingdom
Crabtree Publishing
Maritime House
Basin Road North, Hove
BN41 1WR

Published in Australia
Crabtree Publishing
3 Charles Street
Coburg North
VIC 3058

CONTENTS

WHAT ARE MYTHS?

Myths are ancient stories that passed through many generations of a civilization **by way of spoken and written language. For the Ancient Egyptian people, their myths answered questions about the creation of the world, human existence, and the meaning of life. In answering these questions, the myths reflected the** religion **and beliefs of the Ancient Egyptians. Through their myths, Egyptians learned how to behave and what to value.**

Ancient Egyptian myths offer clues about how the Egyptians viewed their world and what was important to them. Often only pieces of myths have survived as parts of magical spells or prayers. There are fewer complete myths from Ancient Egypt than from Ancient Greece or Rome. But these clues do offer a wonderful view of Egyptian life and beliefs.

Right: The Rosetta Stone is made of basalt and bears inscriptions, from the bottom up, in Ancient Greek, cursive Egyptian, and Egyptian hieroglyphs.

ROSETTA STONE

The Rosetta Stone was discovered in Egypt in 1799 C.E. The writings on the stone slab date back to 196 B.C.E., and are in **demotic**, and hieroglyphic Egyptian, and Ancient Greek. In 1822, Jean-François Champollion broke the code by using the Greek text to decipher the **hieroglyphs**.

The myths reveal that Ancient Egyptians believed in an **afterlife**; the importance of justice; in good over evil; and in the power of gods and kings. These beliefs explain why the **pyramids** were built; why tombs were elaborately decorated and furnished; and why bodies were preserved, or **mummified**, and placed in beautifully designed coffins.

Egyptians honored the natural world and believed their gods were responsible for bringing order to it. They worshiped their gods so that the Sun would rise every day and the Nile River would flood each year. In the myths, gods were shown to be present in the daily lives of kings, princes, priests, craftspeople, peasants, and slaves. Myths of battles and **trade**, birth and death, prove that Egyptians believed that the gods were involved in all aspects of life.

READING ANCIENT SYMBOLS

Although the myths were written thousands of years ago, it was not until about 190 years ago that hieroglyphs—the Ancient Egyptian writing system used on religious documents—were finally decoded. Now that hieroglyphs can be read, connections can be made between what was written and the meaning and importance of the objects and buildings the Egyptians left behind. Today, the influence of Egyptian myths is seen in modern movies, books, art, architecture, fashion, music, and even video games. In some ways, a little piece of myth endures when the **scarab** beetle —a form of the Sun god, **Ra**— appears in a piece of modern jewelry. Myths come alive in the chase scene featuring statues of **Anubis**, the jackal-headed god of the dead, in the 2006 movie *Night at the Museum*. Egyptian myths live on today.

Left: The Ancient Egyptians wrote in hieroglyphs. Each symbol represents a letter, group of letters, word, or an entire idea.

ANCIENT EGYPT

Ancient Egypt is one of the world's oldest civilizations. It began around 3100 B.C.E. It is also among the longest-lasting civilizations, developing slowly and continuing for more than 3,000 years. Today, clues and evidence of its glorious past still exist.

When people think of Ancient Egypt today, they might imagine the **pharaoh** (king), Ramesses the Great (King Ramesses II), storming across the land in his horse-drawn chariot. They picture Ra, the Sun god, soaring across the sky in his solar (Sun-related) boat. They think of the pyramids and the hieroglyphs written on **papyrus**—an early type of paper—or on tomb walls. But for thousands of years, people knew very little about Ancient Egypt. Much of its past was forgotten, hidden, or destroyed. People today can imagine Ancient Egypt because of the modern discoveries that have been made. **Archaeologists** continue to uncover ancient buried secrets.

THE LAND BY THE NILE

Much of Ancient Egypt's history was shaped by its location and climate. The country lies in North East Africa, to the south of the Mediterranean Sea. As it is today, Ancient Egypt was almost entirely covered in sandy desert. The Nile River made it possible for Ancient Egyptians to live and flourish in their hot dry climate. Egyptians depended on the Nile for its annual flood that left behind rich fertile soil for farming. No wonder they believed it to be a gift from the gods.

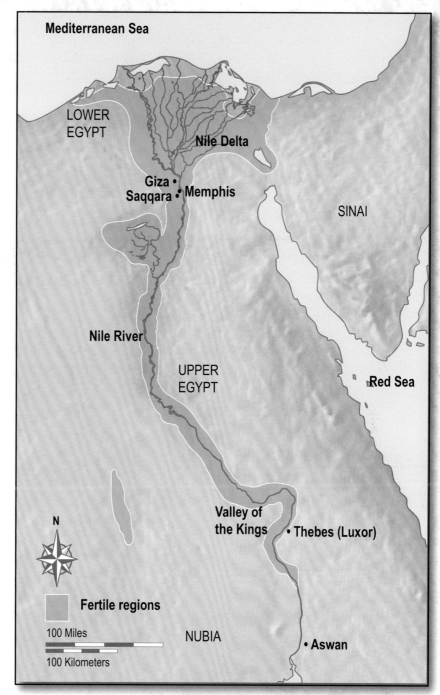

Below: The famous Great **Sphinx** (below left) and Khafre's pyramid (below) lie in Giza, on the west bank of the Nile, outside the modern Egyptian capital Cairo.

Mediterranean Sea

LOWER EGYPT

Nile Delta

Giza
Saqqara • Memphis

SINAI

Nile River

UPPER EGYPT

Red Sea

N

Valley of the Kings

• Thebes (Luxor)

Fertile regions

100 Miles

100 Kilometers

NUBIA

• Aswan

Above: Egypt consists of a narrow strip of fertile land and vast deserts on either side of the Nile River. The river flows from south to north, out into the Mediterranean Sea.

SETTLING THE LAND

During Egypt's early history, people settled along the banks of the Nile to farm and to build communities. Over time, these communities bonded together to form the two distinct cultures of Upper and Lower Egypt. The "Two Lands" were eventually united around 3100 B.C.E., marking the beginning of ancient civilization in Egypt.

Ancient life along the Nile was bustling with action. Peasants farmed the rich soils in the river valley left behind when the Nile River's floodwaters receded, or drew back. Many boats sailed up and down the water carrying people, animals, and cargo. Egyptians caught fish and birds, and hunted animals.

NEW SOIL FROM THE NILE

Just as the earth mound emerged from water in the myth (below), so did fertile soil appear alongside the Nile after the annual floodwaters subsided. The new soil symbolized Egypt to the people. Where the Nile flood did not reach was the desert—a land of chaos.

FROM CHAOS TO CREATION

Ancient Egyptians believed that their creator made order and balance in the world. Egyptians worked hard to look after the gods so that order would win over chaos every day. They had many myths about how the universe was created. This is one of them.

All that existed in the beginning of time was **Nun**, an endless expanse of watery chaos. The first god, **Atum**, was floating in these waters. He created himself from his own thoughts and emerged from Nun as a mound of earth. From the mound arose Ra, the Sun god, in the first sunrise. Atum sneezed and created Shu, the air god. Then he spat, creating Tefnut, the goddess of moisture. Shu and Tefnut became the parents of Geb, god of Earth, and Nut, the sky goddess. In this way, the universe was created. The dome of the heavens covered the world. Below the earth lay Duat—the **underworld**, or the realm of the dead.

Once, Shu and Tefnut became lost in the waters of chaos. Atum sent his Eye (spirit) to find them. When the Eye returned with his children, Atum wept in thankfulness. His tears turned into the first humans.

Egyptians believed that the gods were at work with every flood, creating order and balance in the world. There were many creation myths in Ancient Egypt, describing how the world, Egypt, and the Nile came into existence. Almost all of them refer to life emerging from the waters of chaos.

Below: An Ancient Egyptian wall painting of around 1250 B.C.E. shows a fisherman pulling his net, while the pilot shouts orders to the rowers.

NARMER PALETTE

The Narmer Palette is a siltstone object inscribed with hieroglyphs. It shows the joining of the Two Lands when Egypt became one land in about 3100 B.C.E. King Narmer is shown wearing the white crown of Upper Egypt on this side of the palette, and the red crown of Lower Egypt on the other side.

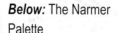

Below: The Narmer Palette

RELIGION

AND GODS

Ancient Egyptians worshiped hundreds of gods and goddesses. They believed that order in the world, or *maat*, would only continue if the gods were constantly honored and praised.

The gods stood for everything that was important to the Egyptians in their daily lives. The gods were also connections with the afterlife, or life after death. For example, there were gods of the sky, the Sun, Earth, the flood, and the desert. There were gods of motherhood, marriage, knowledge, leisure, and death.

In the myths, gods are shown to have behaved like humans. They argued, had battles, threw parties, fell in love, and had children. The gods also had special roles and powers over aspects of the world.

Egyptian kings, called pharaohs, were believed to be sons of the gods. This special connection also meant that pharaohs had important duties to perform for the gods.

Right: The Egyptians believed that the scarab beetle symbolized or represented Khepri, the Sun god Ra in his early morning shape. Khepri rolled the Sun across the sky each day, just as scarabs roll dung for food.

LINK TO TODAY

We are still fascinated by Ancient Egyptian gods and goddesses today, as seen in images of them in modern buildings and in jewelry. Scarab-beetle pendants and winged Isis earrings continue to be fashionable accessories. Statues of Ra and wall art featuring gods and goddesses in Egyptian hieroglyphs are popular decorations in modern homes.

THE NINE GODS

Ancient Egyptians believed in hundreds of gods. Nine of the most important gods were known as the Ennead of Heliopolis. *Ennead* means "group of nine things." *Heliopolis* means "Sun City" and was the center of the worship of Ra, the Sun god. Ra was identified with Atum, the creator god.

The first gods of the Ennead of Heliopolis were Atum and his children, Shu and Tefnut. Tefnut gave birth to Geb, god of Earth, and Nut, goddess of the sky.

Geb and Nut became the parents of the last four gods of the Ennead. These were **Osiris** and his wife **Isis**, and **Seth** and his wife Nephthys. Osiris was the eldest. He was the god of fertility, death, and resurrection (returning to life after death). When Geb retired as king of Egypt's gods, Osiris inherited his father's throne and ruled Egypt wisely. His brother Seth was the god of chaos, storms, and the desert. He was a strong god, who had the head of a strange jackal-like animal with tall square ears.

Isis was one of the most powerful Egyptian goddesses. She was an important mother goddess who knew great magic. She wore the image of a throne on her head and was said to be the mother of the pharaoh. The Egyptians had few myths about her sister Nephthys. According to one myth, Nephthys was the mother of the jackal god, Anubis. Together, Nephthys and Isis protected the dead.

People from each area of Egypt worshiped their own local gods, but some gods were worshiped by everyone across Egypt. The most powerful god of all was Ra, the Sun god and the creator of everything.

To the Ancient Egyptians, the Sun represented the eye of god, watching over them as it blazed across the sky. Over the centuries, and in different regions of Egypt, the Sun god had different names. The name Ra merged, for example, with the name Amun to become Amun-Ra.

Right: In this ancient painting, a dead person prays to the Sun god Ra, shown here with the head of a falcon.

RELIGION AND MAGIC

Religion was closely linked to everyday life in Ancient Egypt. Everyone worshiped the gods. The pharaohs were believed to be the sons of gods and to have direct links to them. Pharaohs built temples where priests cared for the gods. Every day within the temple, a priest would wash, dress, and make offerings to the statue of the god.

Common people were not allowed inside the temples. Instead, they could leave offerings for the gods at local shrines. They asked advice of **oracles**, or statues of the gods. They believed that the oracles could answer questions and give protection and direction in life.

Egyptians also believed in the power of magic. Priests used magic to protect pharaohs and cure people of illnesses.

Above: A tomb relief showing a pharaoh's official, Amenemhat (center), with his family and offerings.

They used wands and spells to carry out their magic for the living and to help the dead in the afterlife. Midwives used magic to aid women in childbirth. **Amulets**, or charms, were worn by the living and dead, and were thought to offer protection and power.

LINK TO TODAY

In Ancient Egypt, words were thought to be very powerful. They were used to activate magic. Today, people value the power of words in songs and books, and when they give or listen to meaningful speeches.

THE SECRET NAME OF RA

Isis knew all the secrets of the world, except Ra's secret name. She longed to know this name and gain the power it held. Through her magic, Isis tricked Ra, but she also cured him. Egyptians believed that magic was just as important as medicine in curing the body.

The Sun god Ra was a drooling old man. One day, Isis gathered up the mud that had been made wet by Ra's spittle. She shaped it into a poisonous snake, which she left at a crossroad. When Ra and his companions came to the crossroad, the snake bit him.

Ra cried out in pain. For a while, the pain was so great that the god could not speak. Finally, he said: "The creature that bit me is not one that I made. I have never known such pain. Gather together the children of the gods, who know magic."

All the children of the gods came before Ra, including Isis. "Tell me your name, divine father," she said. "If I know that, you will be cured." Ra told Isis his many names, but the pain continued. Isis then said: "You have not spoken your real name. If you speak it, the poison will go away." In agony, Ra whispered his secret name into Isis's ear. Isis spoke the magic spell. Ra's pain vanished and Isis now had the enormous power of Ra's secret name.

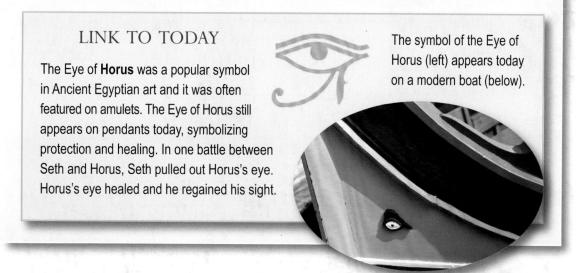

LINK TO TODAY

The Eye of **Horus** was a popular symbol in Ancient Egyptian art and it was often featured on amulets. The Eye of Horus still appears on pendants today, symbolizing protection and healing. In one battle between Seth and Horus, Seth pulled out Horus's eye. Horus's eye healed and he regained his sight.

The symbol of the Eye of Horus (left) appears today on a modern boat (below).

THE FIRST PYRAMID

The most famous and impressive monuments of Ancient Egypt are the pyramids. A king had his pyramid built while he was alive, taking good care of it until it finally became his burial site. He was buried with many treasures and things that would help him in the afterlife.

The first pyramid was King Djoser's Step Pyramid in Saqqara. Its design might have symbolized the steps to heaven for the king to climb. Other theories suggest that pyramids represented the earth mound that first rose out of the waters of chaos when Atum created the world (see page 8).

THE GREAT PYRAMID

King Khufu's Great Pyramid at Giza is one of the Seven Wonders of the Ancient World, and the only wonder still standing. It is the largest of all the pyramids at 479 feet (146 meters) tall. Approximately 2.4 million blocks were used to build the structure.

Pyramid construction involved the efforts of teams of men (not slaves, as previously thought), who worked for the king. Just how the pyramids were constructed is not exactly known, but it is believed that ramps were used to drag blocks upward to build the structure.

Thieves made their way past blocked entrances and robbed the pyramids. In the New Kingdom (1539–1075 B.C.E.), secret rock-cut tombs were hidden in desert cliffs near Thebes, in the Valley of the Kings and the Valley of the Queens. Despite the secret location, robbers found and raided these tombs as well.

LINK TO TODAY

The Step Pyramid of Saqqara and the Great Pyramid of Giza are still popular attractions in modern Egypt. The pyramid design is copied in modern structures throughout the world, such as the Louvre Pyramid in Paris, France, and the Goja Music Hall in Prague in the Czech Republic.

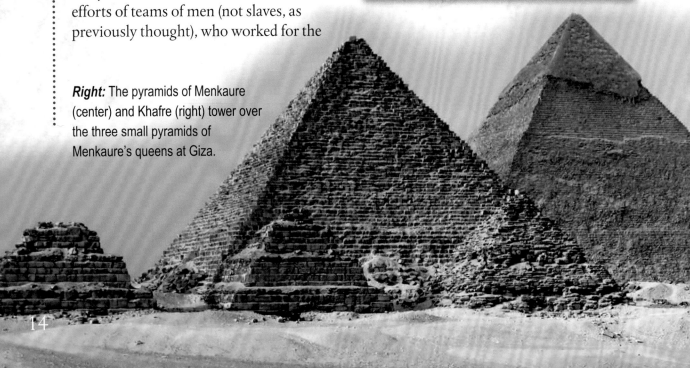

Right: The pyramids of Menkaure (center) and Khafre (right) tower over the three small pyramids of Menkaure's queens at Giza.

THE PRINCE AND THE SPHINX

Dreams were believed to contain important predictions or visions of the future. King Thutmose IV recorded a dream that he had while he was still a prince. The dream was carved on a stela, or stone slab, found between the paws of the Great Sphinx at Giza.

Prince Thutmose liked to take his chariot into the desert to go hunting. One day, he and his companion arrived at a place sacred to the god Horemakhet. This was Giza, where the Great Pyramid and Great Sphinx still stand. In Thutmose's day, the Great Sphinx was mostly buried in sand. The sunshine was very hot, so the prince rested in the shade of the Great Sphinx. He dreamed that Horemakhet appeared and said to him: "Behold me, my son. I am your father." The god promised Thutmose that he would become king if he cleared away the sand.

Thutmose awoke and declared that he would make offerings to the god. Unfortunately, the inscription on the stela is broken here, so the story is unfinished. However, it is known that Prince Thutmose became King Thutmose IV and cleared away the sand, building a wall to guard the Great Sphinx from the desert sands.

GREAT SPHINX

The Great Sphinx is 66 feet (20 m) high and 241 feet (73 m) long. It was carved from limestone near the Great Pyramid of Khufu. It represents a god with the body of a lion and the head of a king.

Right: King Thutmose IV, who ruled from 1401 to 1391 B.C.E., rescued the Great Sphinx from the sand.

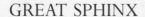

Right: The Great Sphinx sits on the ground near the pyramids at Giza.

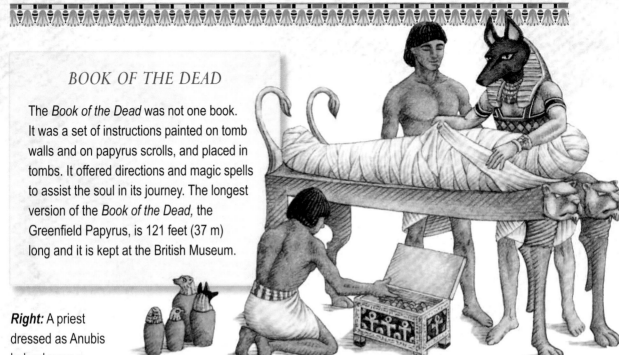

Right: A priest dressed as Anubis helped wrap a mummy. The four jars nearby held the dead person's internal organs.

DEATH AND THE AFTERLIFE

The way that the Ancient Egyptians dealt with death reveals the strong beliefs that they held about the afterlife. According to their religious beliefs, the soul moved through a series of difficult and dangerous tests in the underworld. If the soul passed these tests, it could move on to the Field of Reeds, a paradise of everlasting life.

Egyptians believed that, the body of the dead person had to be mummified, or preserved by drying for the soul to move on to the afterlife. The body was **embalmed,** then wrapped in linen bandages. Jewelry and amulets were set into the bandages. The mummy was then placed in a human-shaped case that was painted to resemble the dead person.

THE RITUALS OF DEATH

Priests performed rituals such as the "opening of the mouth" ceremony, by touching the mummy's face. This would awaken the soul of the dead person so that it could move on toward the afterlife. Egyptians believed that Anubis, god of the dead, oversaw every part of the funeral process.

The coffin was placed in a tomb filled with furniture, food, tools, and other items that would be of use to the dead person in the afterlife. The walls of the tomb were decorated with paintings and writings that helped the soul reach the underworld. Only royal families and wealthy Egyptians could afford very elaborate funerals and tombs.

At first, only pharaohs were thought to move on to the afterlife, but it later was believed that anyone could pass on to the Field of Reeds if they passed the tests of the underworld (see page 17).

JOURNEY INTO THE AFTERLIFE

Ancient Egyptians believed that after death, the soul could move on to the afterlife. To help it get there, a dead person was buried with spells and maps that offered protection, clues, and directions for navigation through the underworld.

The soul fought off attacks by demons. To board the ferry of the underworld, the soul had to name every part of the magic boat and know the name of the man who steered it. The soul then passed many demons guarding gates. By speaking all their names, the soul could pass them. Finally, in the Hall of Two Truths, with Osiris watching from his throne, the soul had to name each of the 42 judges and to deny having committed certain crimes. The soul had to defend itself and convince the judges of its innocence.

Anubis, the jackal-headed god, conducted the final test: He weighed the heart. If the heart weighed more than a feather, the symbol of truth, the soul died a gruesome final death. But if the heart was equal in weight to the feather, the soul moved on to the Field of Reeds—a paradise of plentiful foods, celebration, and everlasting life.

Right: A two-part coffin of an Ancient Egyptian priestess. The mummy has been placed in the bottom piece (right) and a beautifully painted image of the priestess is shown on the top section.

THE NATURAL WORLD

The Nile River was the center of life and activity for the Ancient Egyptians. Everyone depended on the annual flood for successful harvests.

Nothing could grow in the hot and dry desert, called the Red Land. But, once a year, the rains far to the south of Egypt made the Nile waters rise and flood. As the water level finally dropped back, it left behind a black fertile soil in the valley called *Kemet*, or Black Land, where peasants farmed.

LINK TO TODAY

Today, the Aswan High Dam controls the waters of the Nile. It ensures that crops do not get damaged by too much or not enough river water. The dam also produces hydroelectric power for use in towns and cities.

Below: **Scribes** (top right) record the harvest that the farmers (below) have brought in.

18

THE THREE SEASONS

Based on the flood cycle, the Egyptians created a calendar with three predictable seasons. The flood season, *Akhet*, lasted from July to October. The planting season, *Peret*, lasted from November to March. The harvest season, *Shemu*, lasted from April until June. If a flood did not bring water, this caused drought and famine. Too much water destroyed crops. A good flood was seen as a reward from Hapi, god of the Nile. Egyptians also honored Osiris, god of fertility, for the seasons and thanked Isis for the flood.

Below: Hathor (left) was the goddess of fertility and daughter of Ra.

THE WRATH OF RA

Ra was responsible for the sunlight, which was why Egyptians worshiped him. When humans plotted against Ra, he became angry, but then he showed them mercy. In this myth, Ra sent out orders to flood the fields with beer to save humanity. In a similar way, Egyptians felt that the annual flood of the Nile offered them the gift of life through good soil and plentiful harvests.

As Ra grew old, humans plotted to overthrow him. This made Ra very angry. He called a meeting of the gods and asked the advice of Nun, the god of watery chaos. Nun told Ra to send out his Eye to frighten the rebels. So Ra sent out his Eye in the form of the goddess **Hathor**.

Hathor became Sekhmet, the fierce lioness and goddess of war. She stormed across the land and destroyed the rebels. By night, she returned to Ra with the plan to finish the job the next day. But Ra wished to rule over the remaining humans. He had to stop Hathor from continuing her destruction.

As Hathor slept, Ra ordered slave girls to brew beer, which was dyed red. The red beer was then poured into the fields. In the morning, Hathor raced back out with a thirst for blood. But she stopped when she reached the fields that were flooded with a red liquid. It looked just like blood. She lapped up every last drop. The beer made Hathor so drunk, she could not recognize humans anymore. She became peaceful again and the humans were saved.

MURDER AND RESURRECTION OF OSIRIS

The god Osiris was a great mythical king of Egypt. The death and rebirth of Osiris symbolized the same pattern seen in nature, in the seasonal cycles and in the harvests. As god of fertility, Osiris was often shown with green skin, symbolizing vegetation and growth.

When Osiris became king, he taught the Egyptians how to grow crops. He gave them laws. He showed them how to worship the gods. When he was finished with Egypt, he civilized the whole world. But Osiris's jealous brother Seth would stop at nothing to steal the throne.

One day, Seth secretly measured Osiris's body and had a beautiful box made to fit him exactly. Then he tricked Osiris to lie down in it. Once Osiris was inside, Seth's companions sealed the lid. They carried the box secretly to the Nile River and pushed it in, murdering Osiris.

Isis, the wife of Osiris, searched for the box. She traveled all the way to the city of Byblos, in Syria. Here she obtained the box from the king who had found it, and returned the box to Egypt. She hid it in a swamp while she visited her young son Horus. Seth found Osiris's body and cut it into pieces. He scattered the pieces throughout Egypt. As Isis searched for the pieces of Osiris's body, she held ceremonies in his honor, making him a more popular god than Seth.

Isis found all the pieces except one, for which she made a clay replica. When Osiris was restored to life, he taught Horus the art of war. In that way, Horus would be ready to defeat Seth in battle, if Seth became king instead of Horus.

DEATH AND REBIRTH

It was very important for Isis to find the body of her husband Osiris, so his soul could move from it and into the role of king of the dead in the afterlife. The Egyptians believed that the body was where the soul lived, even after death. This is reflected in the Ancient Egyptian practice of preserving and caring for dead bodies.

Above: This painted wooden model shows an Ancient Egyptian farmer plowing his small plot of land with the help of two oxen. The model dates to around 2050 B.C.E.

AGRICULTURE AND HARVESTS

Most of the population were peasant farmers who worked the land alongside the Nile. Some farmers worked on their own small plots of land. Others worked the land owned by the king, who paid the workers by offering them part of the harvest.

During the planting season, women and men broke the land using wooden ax-like tools, or with the aid of oxen that pulled plows. They sprinkled seeds in the fields. To store water needed to irrigate, or artifically water, the land, Egyptians created pools that fed water through channels into the fields. A device called a *shaduf* was used to scoop and move water onto the land.

Harvests yielded many fruits and vegetables, including grapes, melons, figs, cucumbers, and lettuce. Grain crops grown were wheat and barley. **Flax** was grown to make linen. Farmers harvested grain by cutting the stalks with wooden sickles.

Papyrus reeds grew in the marshes along the Nile. Egyptians used them to create a paper-like material called *papyrus*.

FISHING AND HUNTING

Fishing and hunting along the Nile were popular activities. The waterway also provided Ancient Egyptians with a quick and easy transport route.

Fishermen and hunters used simple boats made from papyrus reeds. They pushed the boat through the water using long poles.

Below: Sailors control a wooden boat under full sail on the Nile. This is a detail from a wall painting in the tomb of Sennefer, mayor of Thebes and overseer of fields and cattle of the god Amun.

LINK TO TODAY

Tourists can still sail along the Nile today, just as the Ancient Egyptians did thousands of years ago. *Feluccas* glide naturally on the river carried along by the breeze and the current. Larger motorized cruise ships make stops so tourists can visit major attractions, such as temples and tombs.

Right: Wind-powered feluccas sail along the Nile River.

Many types of fish lived in the Nile. Fishermen used nets, traps, or spears to catch them. People ate fresh fish, or they salted and preserved them to eat later.

Hunters used throwsticks to hunt geese, ducks, and other water birds in the marshes. They used spears to hunt hippopotamuses that posed a danger to sailors and fishermen. A hippo hunt was also a sport that symbolized taking power over evil, just as the god Horus defeated the evil god Seth in their mythical battle.

Larger boats belonged to royal families and were used for transporting items for trade. Some of these boats were made from acacia and sycamore trees that grew along the Nile. Other boats were constructed of wood brought to Egypt from Lebanon.

THE JOURNEY OF THE SUN GOD

Order in the world could never be taken for granted. Egyptians looked after the gods to keep them happy, so that the Sun would rise each day. In his boat, the Sun god worked hard every night to battle the forces of chaos. Boats often appeared in Egyptian myths as ways for the gods, or the souls of the dead, to travel.

Each dawn, the god Khepri took the form of a scarab beetle and pushed the disk of the Sun over the eastern horizon. Then the Sun became the falcon-headed god Ra, who blazed westward across the sky for 12 hours in the day boat. By nightfall, as Ra arrived at the western horizon, he became the ram-headed god Ra-Atum. He and his crew boarded the night boat and plunged into the underworld. The flaming boat cut through the 12 regions of darkness and chaos for another 12 hours. In the first hour, the dead greeted the arrival of the Sun into their world.

By the fifth hour, the crew faced their worst enemy, Apophis, the most dangerous serpent of the entire underworld. Gods held Apophis back as Ra joined with Osiris in the sixth hour. Apophis attacked in the 10th hour, but the gods threw nets over him and tied him up. In the 11th hour, they cut Apophis into pieces.

In the 12th hour, the Sun appeared on the eastern horizon. In the early morning, the beetle pushed the Sun disk over the horizon and Ra rose. Order had been restored for another day, and life could continue.

THOTH PERSUADES TEFNUT

Many Egyptian gods were represented in myths as animals or part-animals. In this myth, the goddess Tefnut, having argued with her father and ran away from Egypt, turned herself into a lioness. The gods Thoth and Shu became baboons so that, in their animal disguises, they could persuade Tefnut to come back to Egypt.

Tefnut had a terrible argument with Ra, her father. She ran away to live in a land far to the south of Egypt. There she changed herself into a lioness. Ra missed his daughter terribly. Not only did he love her, but she was an important guardian for the old god. Ra sent the gods Shu and Thoth to find her. They disguised themselves as baboons and went in search of Tefnut.

When they found Tefnut, she threatened to kill them. Thoth reminded her that the god of fate, Shia, punishes every crime. This made Tefnut pause. Thoth described the beautiful land of Egypt, which she had left behind. Now and then, Tefnut's temper flared, so Thoth began to tell her fables to calm her.

In one of these fables, a lion met up with a leopard, a bear, and a lioness. Each of these other animals had been trapped. The lion could not imagine who could do this to such strong creatures. When they told him that a man was to blame, the lion went hunting for this human. Along the way, the lion met a mouse. Because he was in a bad mood, the lion was about to kill the mouse. But the little creature promised to someday help the lion, if only the lion would let him live. This promise made the lion laugh, because it seemed so silly. The lion let the mouse go and went on to find bigger game—the human. Soon the lion fell into a pit and got tangled in a net. He, too, had been trapped by the man! The man hauled the lion out of the pit and tied him up. That night, the little mouse came along and chewed through the lion's bonds. Free, the grateful lion ran away with the mouse.

Tefnut knew the moral of this tale, so she did not harm Thoth. The god persuaded Tefnut to return home to her father. When she arrived in Egypt, Tefnut turned into the much friendlier goddess, Hathor.

ANIMALS

Animals were of great importance to the Ancient Egyptians. They were a source of food and clothing and they worked on farms. Animals were also thought to be sacred and to symbolize the gods. Some myths featured gods changing into animals and taking on their powers (see page 24). Egyptians also adored animals. Cats, dogs, and even monkeys were kept as pets. When they died, pets were often mummified.

LINK TO TODAY

The Lion and the Mouse of the Thoth myth (on page 24) is a story that has been told over and over throughout the centuries. It continues to be told today in books, plays, and cartoons. We still appreciate its message that the small and physically weak can help the strong and powerful.

Left: This wooden funeral model dating from around 1950 B.C.E., shows the porch of a private house. Family and scribes are observing and counting the cattle walking by.

DAILY LIFE

Ancient Egyptian society was like a pyramid, with the king at the very top. The upper classes held the most powerful positions, but were few in number. The many peasants were at the base of the social pyramid.

The king and his family held the highest position in Egyptian society. The king acted as the country's ruler and head priest. He was also the judge and army leader. He conducted most of his business in the throne room of his palace. A king was almost always the son of a former king.

Women held leadership roles and sometimes even ruled the country. A woman gained a leadership role through her relationship with the king. Hatshepsut and Cleopatra were queens of Egypt.

The next level down in Egyptian society was the educated nobility and the king's close attendants, such as the high priest, **viziers**, medical staff, and scribes.

Right: The boy king Tutankhamun reigned for just 10 years, beginning around 1332 B.C.E. Here, he is shown with his wife Ankhesenamun.

BURIED TOMBS

In 1922, archaeologist Howard Carter found the tomb of the pharaoh Tutankhamun, who became the king of Egypt at the age of eight and lived to be just 18. Although the tomb had been robbed years before, most of its contents were left intact. The treasures found within Tutankhamun's tomb have been on exhibit in museums around the world.

The middle class held the next rank in the social pyramid. They consisted of local priests, merchants, skilled craftspeople, and musicians. Lower down again were the farmers, peasants, and soldiers who made up the largest group of the population. Only servants and slaves were below them. Getting an education, although difficult for peasants, was one of the only ways for Egyptians to move up this social pyramid.

THE ELOQUENT PEASANT

Justice was highly regarded among all classes in Egyptian society. This story reveals that all people could count on good winning over evil. The peasant's beautiful language is what helped him receive the justice he deserved after an evil man stole his donkey and his goods.

A poor peasant named Khun-Anup traveled with his donkeys toward the market. He hoped to trade some goods for food to give to his hungry family. A crafty man saw the peasant coming. He tricked the peasant and stole the donkeys and goods.

Khun-Anup looked for the high steward, Rensi, to ask for his help. He explained how he was tricked and his possessions stolen. Khun-Anup's words were so poetic that Rensi was stunned by their beauty.

Rensi did not, however, agree to judge Khun-Anup's case. The peasant continued to speak more powerful words. He compared Rensi to the god Ra, who provided for his people. After nine days, Khun-Anup threatened to tell the god Anubis that Rensi was not doing his duty. Rensi backed down and gave Khun-Anup justice. He also sent the peasant's poetry to the palace for the king to enjoy.

Right: These bakers preparing bread were from a class of people near the bottom of Egypt's social pyramid. Only slaves and servants were below this class.

A LIFE OF WORK

The daily lives of Ancient Egyptians revolved around work. From the duties of the king, his priests, and court attendants right down to the peasants working the fields, all Egyptian jobs were specialized and all required different skills.

The king was supported in his duties by viziers, government officials, and high priests. Scribes held powerful positions as record-keepers and writers of government documents and religious scripts. Usually, only a few privileged boys had the opportunity to learn to read and write and to undergo the training to become a scribe. Thoth, the god of knowledge, was also the god of writing.

Craftspeople created practical and beautiful objects for Egyptians. Some craftworkers made mud bricks for homes or linen to make clothing from flax. Carpenters made furniture, boats, and coffins using saws and chisels. Potters created bowls for everyday use and fancy vases for decoration.

Artisans created beautiful jewelry of beads or more valuable pieces made from gold and precious gemstones. Skilled artists painted tomb walls for royal or noble families.

Aside from farming, peasants also ground grain and made bread. They brewed beer and made wine from grapes. They also sold food in the market.

Above: This scribe, who dates from around 2500 B.C.E., is sitting cross-legged, ready to write something down in a document.

THE GOD PTAH

Egyptians worshiped Ptah as the god of craftspeople, including jewelers, potters, artisans, and those who worked on the royal tombs. Ptah was also one of the gods associated with the creation of the world. It was believed that he planned the creation of the universe and spoke his plan into action.

THE INTELLIGENT THIEF

Pharaohs cherished their possessions made by the hands of skilled craftspeople. They also valued intelligence. This myth exaggerates the value of intelligence when a pharaoh rewards a clever thief who was able to break into his heavily guarded and sealed storage building. In reality, thieves in Egypt were punished for their crimes.

A rich pharaoh had so many treasures that he ordered an architect to make a special building to keep his valuables safe from thieves. The treasures seemed very safe because the building had no windows, the door was sealed shut, and guards watched over it day and night.

Years later, as the architect was dying, he told his two sons that he had built a secret entrance to the building. He instructed his sons on how to enter. Each night, the sons entered the king's building unseen by the guards. Little by little, the thieves stole the king's treasures.

When the pharaoh visited his building, he noticed some things missing. He thought this was impossible because there were no windows, the door was sealed, and he trusted his guards. The thief was obviously very clever, so the king set a trap.

That night, as the thieves stole from the king, one brother got caught in the trap. He told the other brother to cut off his head so the king could not identify the body. When the king discovered the headless body, he hoped the thief's family would come to claim it, but the living brother cleverly stole that, too.

The pharaoh wanted such a clever man on his side. He offered his daughter's hand in marriage if the thief would come forward. The thief accepted the pharaoh's offer and, in return, offered him his intelligence for many years.

Right: This pendant, made of gold inlaid with glass and semiprecious stones, takes the shape of a falcon with outstretched wings. The falcon is the symbol of the gods Ra and Horus.

THE DIVINE BIRTH OF HATSHEPSUT

Egypt prospered under the rule of the female pharaoh Hatshepsut. The scenes of Hatshepsut's birth are found in her temple at Deir el-Bahri. It is believed that this myth defended Hatshepsut's position and right to rule as a woman.

The king of the gods, Amun, foretold that there would be a female pharaoh in Egypt. Thoth, the god of wisdom, told Amun that Queen Ahmose should be the child's mother. Amun disguised himself as Ahmose's husband, King Thutmose II, and visited the queen one night. He informed the queen that she was chosen to be the mother of a divine daughter, Hatshepsut (see page 31).

(see page 31)

Amun then met with the ram-headed creator god, Khnum. Based on Amun's instructions, Khnum created Hatshepsut out of clay on his potter's wheel.

When it was time for Ahmose to give birth, Khnum and Heket, the frog-headed goddess of childbirth, led Ahmose to the room where Hatshepsut was born. Amun welcomed his daughter and proclaimed her the pharaoh of Egypt.

FAMILY LIFE

The family was at the core of Ancient Egyptian daily life. After a couple married, they were expected to raise a family. They used spells and prayers in hopes of being blessed with children. People worshiped the goddesses Isis and Hathor for their links to the powers of fertility, childbirth, and motherhood.

Within families, boys of all classes helped their fathers at work, and trained in similar trades or positions. Girls helped their mothers in their daily work, and with the cooking. Boys of the upper classes were educated by scribes, priests, or other

Below: This wooden model shows what the mud-brick house of a farm manager would have looked like in the 1900s B.C.E.

teachers. Girls of the upper classes learned to play an instrument, sing, or dance. It is thought that some of them learned to read and write. They were sometimes trained to become priestesses.

Clothing was usually made of white linen. Lower classes wore simple kilts and dresses. Upper classes wore more elaborate dresses with capes and shawls, along with jewelry and scented wigs. Both men and women wore make-up. Children had shaved heads with a braided lock remaining on one side. The lock was known as the "sidelock of youth."

HOUSES AND BUSINESSES

Most people lived in mud-brick homes built on high ground to avoid the threat of floods. Houses of the upper classes were also made from mud bricks, but they had many rooms containing beautifully made furniture and fancy decorations.

Ancient Egyptian women had many rights and were more empowered than the women of other ancient countries. They could run businesses and work in many jobs. They could even own their own land. If they were unhappy in their marriages, they could divorce their husbands.

LINK TO TODAY

Ancient Egyptian women worshiped Hathor as the goddess of fertility, childbirth, and motherhood. She was often associated with the sacred cow and was depicted as a woman with cow ears, or as a woman with cow horns with a Sun disk positioned between them. Women today still visit Hathor's temple at Dendera in hopes of being blessed with pregnancy.

Right: This woman is wearing her finest clothes, most notably a pleated dress.

HATSHEPSUT

When King Thutmose II died in 1479 B.C.E., his son Thutmose III was very young. So Thutmose II's wife, Hatshepsut, ruled Egypt for 21 years while he grew up. Although women held important roles in society, Hatshepsut presented herself as a man.

LEISURE AND ENTERTAINMENT

Ancient Egyptians liked to have fun. They played sports and games, listened to music, danced, feasted, and threw parties (see page 33). Children played with wooden toys, balls, and dolls. Both children and adults enjoyed board games such as *senet*.

People enjoyed the Nile for swimming and leisure boating. Along with fishing and hunting for sport, wrestling was a very popular activity among young men.

Dancers entertained at royal parties as musicians played flutes, harps, lyres, and lutes. Festivals were celebrated to honor a god or goddess, mark the anniversary of a king's rule, or praise the annual flooding of the Nile.

Below: Senet, or "passing," was a popular board game. In the New Kingdom, the passage of the deceased through the afterlife was sometimes represented by success in games such as senet. In this wall painting, Queen Nefertari is shown playing the game, the board and pieces of which are shown on the right.

Above: Senet game board and playing pieces

KING SNEFERU'S PARTY

Celebration was important to all Egyptians. They enjoyed music, dance, and feasting. They threw parties and attended festivals. When King Sneferu's party was interrupted, his chief priest used magic to keep the party going and make the king happy.

King Sneferu wandered through his palace, trying to find a cure for his boredom. Finally, he called for a priest, Djadja-em-ankh, to help him. He suggested that Sneferu go to the lake in the palace grounds and spend the day watching beautiful women row boats on the lake.

The king loved the idea, so he called for 20 young women. The king soon forgot his boredom as he enjoyed the beauty of the women and the peaceful motion of the oars. The entertainment pleased the king until one of the women stopped rowing.

"Why have you stopped?" the king asked.

"I have lost my turquoise pendant," the woman replied.

The king offered to replace it, but the woman insisted that she wanted the one that she had lost.

Sneferu wanted the fun to continue, so he called for Djadja-em-ankh to find the pendant. The priest used his magic to shift the deep waters so that he could see the bottom of the lake. He scanned the entire area around the boat until a glint caught his eye. It was the turquoise pendant. He pulled the pendant from the water and gave it back to its owner. The king was delighted, and threw another party.

Below: Four Ancient Egyptian musicians play the arched harp, lute, double oboe, and lyre, while a small child dances in between them.

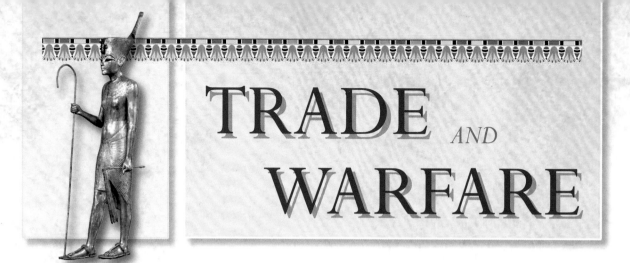

TRADE *AND* WARFARE

When Egyptians needed resources that were not plentiful or available within Egypt, they traveled to other countries by boat or across land to trade for them. Foreigners also visited Egypt to engage in trade.

Imports from abroad included gold, ebony, and ivory from Nubia—a region to the south of Egypt—and cedar wood from Lebanon. From the distant Red Sea land of Punt came incense, myrrh, and baboons, and from Afghanistan came lapis lazuli (a blue stone). Egypt exported linen, papyrus, gold, vases, grain, and other foods.

Gold was imported and exported because Egyptians prized the precious metal and made great use of it. Gold was considered the gleaming metal of the gods. It was an important material used to make treasures for the kings' tombs. On mummy cases, gold represented the skin of the gods. It was also used to make jewelry and ornaments for the upper classes.

LINK TO TODAY

Gold continues to be seen as a symbol of wealth in modern society. It is used to make jewelry, plaques, and artwork, as well as some coins and medals. Investors buy and sell gold in the stock markets around the world. India and China are two of the biggest consumers of gold.

Left: The land of Punt lay to the south of Egypt, along the Red Sea. Here, some men from Punt are bringing gifts for the trade expedition from Egypt.

THE SHIPWRECKED SAILOR

This myth highlights the idea that everything happens for a reason. The serpent god rewarded the shipwrecked sailor for his honesty, as Egyptians believed that good deeds pleased the gods.

Returning home from a long journey, a sailor said to one of the king's attendants: "I need to tell you the story of my journey. I sailed toward the pharaoh's mines on a very large ship with 150 sailors. But a storm set in. Huge waves broke our boat apart. I grabbed a piece of wood, but all the other sailors drowned. A giant wave swept me on to an island. I rested in the shade of the trees and found plenty of food to eat.

"Then a long serpent with a pharaoh's beard slithered toward me. 'Why did you come to this island?,' it said. 'Speak the truth now or you shall disappear like a flame that is blown out.'

"I told the serpent how a wave swept me onto the island. The serpent said, 'Have no fear. You have survived, so the gods must have planned it this way. You will stay here for four months until a ship comes and takes you back home.' Then I praised the serpent god and said, 'I will tell the king about you and return one day with gifts fit for a god!' But the serpent replied, 'I already have such things. After you leave, you can never return because this island will disappear into the waves.'

"Just as the serpent god foretold, a ship came for me. As it approached, the god wished me well and asked me to speak highly of him. He gave me many gifts that I must now present to the pharaoh."

THE POWER OF GOLD

People went to great lengths to serve and honor the gods and pharaohs. Most of the goods Ancient Egyptians imported from other countries were the raw materials they needed to make beautiful objects for the gods, or for pharaohs to use in the afterlife. After people traveled great distances for goods, just as the sailors did, more long hours of work were endured by craftspeople who created the finished items for the gods and pharaohs.

THE GIRL WITH THE RED ROSE SLIPPERS

Slaves were sometimes able to win their freedom. The rich merchant sympathized with the young slave girl's circumstances and tried to offer her a better life. This shows that harmony and respect existed between the classes.

One day, a slave girl stood on display in the village during a slave sale. When the rich merchant, Charaxos, first saw the girl, he was stunned by her beauty. He offered the highest bid and bought her. Once alone with the beautiful girl, he listened to her story.

Her name was Rhopodis and she told Charaxos that pirates stole her from her homeland in northern Greece. A rich man bought her and waited for her to grow up so he could sell her again. Charaxos felt bad for what the girl had gone through, so he gave her a big house to live in with gardens and a pool in the yard. He often sent Rhopodis precious gifts and treated her like a princess. Rhopodis loved every gift she received, but she cherished her red rose slippers the most. She wore them every day and admired every step she took in them.

One day, while swimming, Rhopodis was shocked to see an eagle sweep down and scoop up one of her red slippers left at the edge of the pool. As Rhopodis wept, the eagle soared all the way to the courtyard of Pharaoh Amasis and dropped the slipper in his lap. Surprised, Amasis lifted the pretty slipper and knew immediately that it must belong to a beautiful girl. The pharaoh sent messengers all across Egypt in search of the owner of the shoe.

Finally, the messengers found Rhopodis. She tried on the slipper and it fitted perfectly. Rhopodis showed the messengers the matching slipper that the eagle had left behind and was taken to meet the pharaoh. It was not long before she became his queen.

LINK TO TODAY

Similar stories of a poor girl, who loses a slipper that is found by a prince, have been told over the centuries. Today we enjoy versions of this story featuring Cinderella.

CAPTURING SLAVES

Slaves had the lowest status on the social pyramid. Many came to Egypt as prisoners of war while others were sold in trade. When the Egyptian army took captives in war, it was a symbol of Egypt's power and dominance over her enemies. Many slaves were brought back to Egypt from Nubia. Prisoners of war often became Egyptian soldiers and could even attain a high rank in the army. It was one of the ways that a slave could eventually earn freedom.

Slaves also worked for kings in mines, and in royal workshops or on farm land. Some slaves worked in the homes of the upper classes. A slave could be set free by his or her owner.

SEKHMET

The lion-headed goddess of war, Sekhmet, was revered for her protective powers in battle. She was the wife of Ptah and the daughter of Ra, whom she supported against his enemies. She was thought to be dangerous and threatening. These were qualities that the Egyptian kings wanted their armies to portray in war.

Below: Slaves worked as maids in the households of their owners. Here, two slaves are decorating the mistress of the house with jewelry that she can then wear at a banquet.

SOLDIERS AND WAR

The highest ranks in the army were held by the educated classes, noblemen, and family members of the pharaoh. Soldiers who proved themselves in war, however, could move up the ranks of the army.

Egypt did not have a highly organized army until the end of the Middle Kingdom. The first Egyptian soldiers fought on foot carrying axes, spears, and shields. By the beginning of the New Kingdom, soldiers used horse-drawn chariots upon which they would charge toward their enemy with great speed, armed with bows and arrows. Egyptians also used warships to fight battles on the Nile and to transport troops.

One conflict involved the Egyptian desire to gain control over Nubian gold supplies. Another conflict with the Hittite army led to a famous chariot battle at Kadesh in Syria around 1275 B.C.E. King Ramesses II claimed to have defeated the Hittite army by himself, with only a few soldiers who loyally remained by his side.

During the New Kingdom, Egypt maintained control and influence over a large and expanding empire. By the end of this period, internal conflicts mounted between nobles and priests. Civil wars broke out. The country became less stable and was ruled by foreign kings. Eventually, Egypt was conquered by Rome.

Below: Wearing a blue crown and protected by vulture goddesses flying overhead, Tutankhamun charges his Syrian enemies in battle. This dramatic scene comes from a painted wooden chest in his tomb in the Valley of the Kings near Thebes.

THE BATTLE OF HORUS AND SETH

Seth murdered his brother, Osiris, who was king of Egypt. Seth demanded that the other gods crown him king. Horus, the son of Osiris, knew that he had to defeat Seth to take the throne. Horus sought justice and revealed that good can overcome evil.

After Seth murdered Osiris, the gods quarreled about who should be the king. Thoth, the god of wisdom, told Atum that Horus, Osiris's son, should get the crown. Ra, the Sun god, thought that Osiris's brother Seth should become king because Seth was a full-grown man.

Horus's mother, Isis, even tricked Seth into admitting that a son should inherit his father's possessions. But Seth refused to give up the throne without a fight. He challenged Horus to a battle. Both gods turned themselves into hippopotamuses and fought in the river. Isis threw a spear at the one she thought was Seth, but she injured her son by mistake. Then she struck Seth. But she felt so bad for wounding her brother that she let him go. Horus was furious with his mother and cut off her head. The gods had to replace it with the head of a cow.

Horus fled to the hills to avoid punishment for his crime. Seth caught up with Horus and tore out his eyes. When Hathor found Horus weeping, she healed him.

Next, Horus challenged Seth to a boat-building contest. Each god had to build a boat of stone. Seth's heavy stone boat sank. But Horus built his boat with wood and coated it with stone-colored paint, so that it floated. Horus won the contest.

The contests between Horus and Seth lasted for 80 years. Thoth advised Atum to write a letter to Osiris, now god of the underworld, to ask him to decide who should be king. Osiris replied: "Why are you trying to deny my son his right? Do I not provide food for all of you gods?" This angered Atum, who had created the universe. But Osiris replied, "If you do not make my son king, I will unleash the demons of the underworld where you journey every night." This threat frightened the gods into agreeing with Osiris that Horus should be king. Seth agreed and Ra rewarded him by making him guardian of his solar boat.

EGYPTIAN LEGACY

Ancient Egyptian gods, goddesses, and symbols continue to have an influence on modern society. Egyptian myths have inspired writers, composers, artists, and moviemakers, throughout history. Aspects of some of these myths are evident even in architecture and fashion.

Egyptian architecture inspires buildings of today, such as the Washington Monument, the Luxor Hotel in Las Vegas, Nevada, and the Pyramid Arena in Memphis, Tennessee. These structures not only reveal the modern fascination with Ancient Egyptian architecture, but they also help people imagine what Ancient Egyptian buildings looked like.

For decades, moviemakers have created Egyptian-themed movies such as *We Want Our Mummy* (1939), *Cleopatra* (1963), *Raiders of the Lost Ark* (1981), *Stargate* (1994), *The Prince of Egypt* (1998), *The Scorpion King* (2002), and *Night at the Museum* (2006). Egyptian gods and goddesses live on in television and cartoon episodes, video games, and board games.

Ancient Egyptian designs continue to make fashion comebacks in serpent necklaces, rings, bangles, women's hairstyles, and the makeup artistry of "Cleopatra eyes."

BURIED ALIVE!
EGYPTIAN FAKIRS OUTDONE

Master Mystifier
HOUDINI
THE GREATEST NECROMANCER OF THE AGE–PERHAPS OF ALL TIMES
The Literary Digest

Left: Harry Houdini was famed for his ability to escape from impossible situations. In 1926, he competed with an Egyptian to see who could be buried alive the longest.

Right: The Luxor Hotel in Las Vegas and, below, the obelisk-shaped Washington Monument in Washington, both show the influence of Egyptian architecture.

LINK TO TODAY

Kids and adults of this century enjoy Egyptian-inspired video games such as *Tomb Raider, Immortal Cities: Children of the Nile,* and *Pharaoh.* Gamers can learn about Egyptian history and mythology while they play. The games feature challenges through tombs, searches for artifacts, and run-ins with the gods and goddesses.

EGYPTOLOGY

Egyptology is the study of the culture, language, and history of Ancient Egypt. Egyptologists continue to study the subject and share their research, including their work related to the gods, myths, and hieroglyphs. They offer inspiration to artists, architects, writers, and readers.

Right: The archaeologist Howard Carter looks at the treasures he discovered in Tutankhamun's tomb at the Valley of Kings near Thebes in 1922.

Students in schools around the world study Ancient Egypt. Kids reading Egyptian myths today can enjoy the timeless themes and messages that Ancient Egyptian children must have been very familiar with.

Museums have permanent and touring exhibits that allow people to get an up-close view of Ancient Egyptian artifacts. Visitors can see how frequently symbols from the myths, such as serpents, the solar boat, or images of the gods, are represented on artifacts.

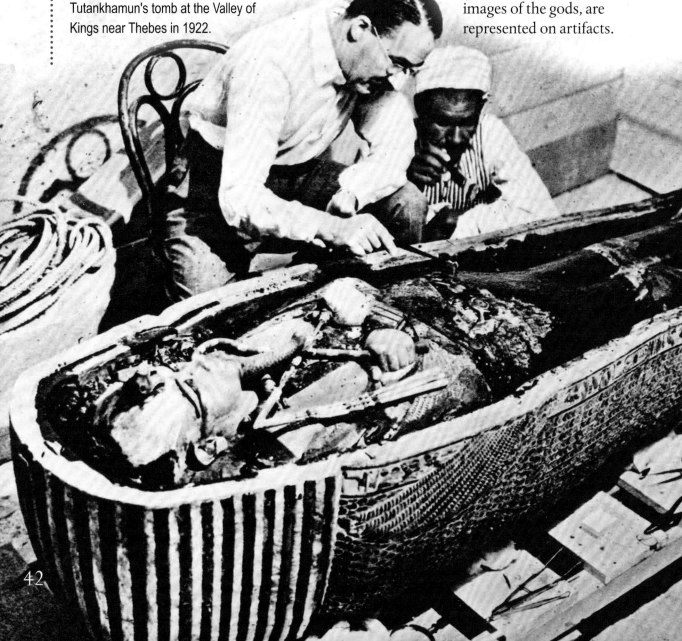

ADMINSTRATION

To build the pyramids of Ancient Egypt, villages to house the workers were set up alongside the construction site. The organization of the workforce and its village required many officials and scribes. This use of civil servants was copied from the Egyptians by the Ancient Greeks and Romans. They also copied the Egyptian system of writing down laws and rules, and used them as the basis of their governments and armies. The administrative skills of the Egyptians are still copied today.

Right: This modern plate, the recent model of a cat, and a girl with her pet cat, are all legacies of the gods and myths of Ancient Egypt. The Ancient Egyptians kept cats as pets and mummified them after death.

ARCHAEOLOGISTS

Archaeologists continue to uncover Egypt's ancient past. A discovery of mummified eagles found in a tomb dating back to about 489 B.C.E. was recently announced. This offers us another clue to understanding what the Egyptians believed about the afterlife and about the sacred significance of animals connected with many of the myths.

LITERATURE, MYTHS, AND EDUCATION

Today, authors write books based on what is known about the tombs of the pharaohs, the mummies within them, and the gods that helped souls journey to the afterlife. They also write about virtues honored by Ancient Egyptians that are still important today: justice, order, goodness, and love.

Ancient Egyptians wrote poetry, love songs, and autobiographies. They exchanged letters and kept written records of legal trials. They left graffiti on walls. They even drew political cartoons.

Today, people still wonder about the beginning of time and how the world came to be, just as the Ancient Egyptians did.

Above: The Egyptian-themed 2001 American adventure movie *The Mummy Returns* was a written and directed by Stephen Sommers.
Left: Ancient Egyptian gods crouch below some hieroglyphs in this wall painting.

People still ask questions about human existence, the stars and planets, the heavens, and the universe. Though there are now scientific explanations for where the Sun goes after it sets, it is fun to imagine that Ra fights Apophis in the underworld so that the Sun can rise in the morning. And as in Ancient Egyptian times, people today are concerned with the afterlife.

NASA PLANS

In 2016, NASA plans to launch a spacecraft—called OSIRIS-REx, after the Egyptian god—to bring asteroid samples back to Earth.

TIME CHART

Before 3100 B.C.E. Pre-dynastic Period
First farming communities settle along the Nile
Stone carvings and wall paintings are first produced

3100–2625 B.C.E. Early Dynastic Period
Unification of Upper and Lower Egypt by King Narmer, also known as Menes,
  who builds the capital city of Memphis
The Palette of Narmer
2650 B.C.E. Step Pyramid at Saqqara built during the reign of King Djoser

2625–2130 B.C.E. Old Kingdom
2580 B.C.E. The Great Pyramid at Giza built during the reign of King Khufu
2530 B.C.E. The Great Sphinx at Giza built

2130–1980 B.C.E. First Intermediate Period
Shorter reigns and new families of kings

1980–1630 B.C.E. Middle Kingdom
Egypt conquers Nubia

1630–1539 B.C.E. Second Intermediate Period

1539–1075 B.C.E. New Kingdom
1539–1069 B.C.E. Tombs dug out in the Valley of the Kings
1479 B.C.E. Reign of Queen Hatshepsut begins
1322 B.C.E. Tutankhamun is buried in the Valley of the Kings
1275 B.C.E. Ramesses II defeats the Hittites at the Battle of Kadesh

1075–664 B.C.E. Third Intermediate Period
Political divisions in Egypt

664–332 B.C.E. Late Period
525 B.C.E. Persians rule Egypt

332–30 B.C.E. Ptolemaic Period
332 B.C.E. Alexander the Great conquers Egypt
30 B.C.E. The end of the reign of Cleopatra, the last Greek ruler of Egypt

30 B.C.E.–today Roman Empire to Modern Times
30 B.C.E. Egypt becomes part of the Roman Empire
395 C.E. Roman rule in Egypt ends
1822 Jean-François Champollion cracks the code of hieroglyphs on the Rosetta Stone
1922 Discovery of Tutankhamun's tomb by Howard Carter

GLOSSARY

afterlife Everlasting life of the soul after death

amulets Charms worn for good luck and protection against evil

Anubis The god of embalming, who weighed the heart in the underworld

archaeologists People who study the past through digging up and examining ancient objects

Atum The creator god, often associated with Ra

civilization A very developed and organized society with cities

demotic A cursive form of Egyptian writing used from about 650 B.C.E.

dynasty A line of kings or pharaohs

embalmed A dead body that has been treated and preserved so it can survive in the afterlife

flax A plant grown and harvested for oils and to make linen cloth

Hathor The goddess of motherhood, fertility, and women

hieroglyphs The symbols and pictures of Ancient Egyptian writing

Horus The falcon-headed god of kings and life

Isis The goddess of love, motherhood, fertility, and magic

mummified A dead body that has been dried, embalmed, and bandaged; the process involved is mummification

Nun The waters of chaos

oracles Statues of gods or goddesses that were consulted for advice

Osiris The god of harvests, fertility, and the underworld

papyrus The paper-like material made from papyrus reeds

pharaoh An Egyptian king

pyramids Stone or mud-brick structures with four sloping sides that meet at a point on the top, often used as burial sites for pharaohs

Ra The Sun god of creation

religion A system of beliefs usually involving prayers and worship of one or more gods and goddesses

scarab A large beetle that served as a symbol of the Sun god

scribes Writers of religious scripts and government documents

Seth The god of the desert, storms, and evil

sphinx A mythical creature with the body of a lion and the head of a human

Thoth The god of knowledge and writing

trade The process of buying and selling goods or services

underworld The place where the Ancient Egyptians believed souls went in the afterlife

viziers Important advisers of the pharaoh

LEARNING MORE

BOOKS

Bell, Michael, and Sarah Quie. *Ancient Egyptian Civilization.* New York: The Rosen Publishing Group, 2010.

Butcher, Kristen. *Pharaohs and Foot Soldiers: One Hundred Ancient Egyptian Jobs You Might Have Desired or Dreaded.* Toronto: Annick Press, 2009.

Challen, Paul. *Life in Ancient Egypt* (Peoples of the Ancient World). St. Catharines, ON: Crabtree Publishing, 2011.

Green, Jen. *Hail! Ancient Egyptians* (Hail! History). St. Catharines, ON: Crabtree Publishing, 2011.

Morley, Jacqueline. *Egyptian Myths.* Chicago: NTC/ Contemporary Publishing Group, Inc., 1999.

Parker, Vic. *Traditional Tales from Ancient Egypt.* North Mankato: Thameside Press, 2000.

Ross, Stewart. *Tales of the Dead: Ancient Egypt.* New York: Dorling Kindersley Ltd., 2003.

Tyldesley, Joyce. *Egypt.* New York: Simon & Schuster Books for Young Readers, 2007.

WEBSITES

BBC History
www.bbc.co.uk/history/ancient/

The British Museum
www.britishmuseum.org/learning/schools_and_teachers/ resources/cultures/Ancient_egypt.aspx

The Egyptian Museum
http://egyptianmuseumcairo.org/

Ancient Egypt: the Mythology
www.egyptianmyths.net/

National Geographic: Explore the Pyramids
www.nationalgeographic.com/pyramids/pyramids.html

[Website addresses correct at time of writing—they can change.]

INDEX